HOW TO ANALYZE PEOPLE

The Definitive Guide to Speed-Reading People Using Behavioral Psychology and Analyzing Body Language

By
Jake Bishops

Table of Contents

Introduction 9

4 Commandments for Reading Body Language 9

Commandment One: Situational Awareness 9

Commandment Two: Context and Baseline 9

Commandment Three: Changes What Never Changes 9

Commandment Four: From Local to Global 10

Chapter 1. How to Analyze People 11

Why Analyze People 12

How to Analyze People 14

When to Analyze People 15

In Parenting 16

In Relationships 16

In the Workplace 16

In Public 17

In Arguments 17

In Self-reflection 18

In Self-regulation 18

Chapter 2. How to Learn Speed-Reading People 19

What Is Speed-Reading? 19

   1. Train Your Eyes to Make Bigger Jumps 20

   2. Go Straight Ahead 20

   3. Stop Speaking the Words 21

   4. Use Skimming Technique 22

   5. Use the Scanning Technique 22

   6. Monitor Your Performance 23

   7. Train Your Focusing Ability 23

   8. Find a Quiet Place to Do Your Reading 25

   9. Do Not Insist When You Are Tired 25

   10. Read Whenever You Can 26

Chapter 3. Understanding Deception and Deceptive Tactics 28

   The Media 28

   Food 28

   Religion 28

   Personal Relationships 29

   The Psychology of Deception 31

   Top Ways to Effectively Deceive 33

      Reasoning Is Everything 34

      Have Your Story All Laid Out 34

Create a Lie That Is Not Completely a Lie 35

Chapter 4. Narcissism in a Relationship 37

Signs of Narcissism in a Relationship 38

They Often Make One Feel Guilty 38

They Are Manipulative 38

Entitlement 39

They Seem to Defy Some Rules That Apply to Everyone 39

Frequent Threats 39

Externally Impressive 40

They Believe They're Very Special 40

Hot and Cold 40

Narcissistic Abuse 41

Workplace 41

Parent-Child 42

Love Relationships 42

Narcissism and Healthy Relationship 44

Respect for Each Other 44

Chapter 5. Victims of the Narcissist 45

Conscientious people 47

People with Empathy 48

People with Integrity 49

People with Resilience 50

Extremely Sentimental People 50

People Who Were Raised in Dysfunctional Environments 51

People with a Frantic Need to Be Loved and Are Lonely 52

People Who Accept Blame Willingly 52

Chapter 6. Attraction and Manipulation - Put This in Correlation 53

Facial Expressions, Features, and Head Movement 55

Playing with Hair and Moving the Head 55

Eye Movement 56

Eyebrow Movement 57

Lips 57

Body and Limb Movements 58

Body Positions 58

Standing Positions 59

Arm Positions 59

Leg and Foot Positions 60

Sitting Positions 60

Chapter 7. Understanding Emotions 62

Chapter 8. Being Proactive 71

Leading by Example 71

Reflecting and Growing 73

Motivating Your Team 74

Increasing Listening Skills... 76

Conclusion **78**

© Copyright 2021 by Jake Bishops - All rights reserved.

This Book is provided with the sole purpose of providing relevant information on a specific topic for which every reasonable effort has been made to ensure that it is both accurate and reasonable. Nevertheless, by purchasing this Book, you consent to the fact that the author, as well as the publisher, are in no way experts on the topics contained herein, regardless of any claims as such that may be made within. As such, any suggestions or recommendations that are made within are done so purely for entertainment value. It is recommended that you always consult a professional prior to undertaking any of the advice or techniques discussed within.

This is a legally binding declaration that is considered both valid and fair by both the Committee of Publishers Association and the American Bar Association and should be considered as legally binding within the United States.

The reproduction, transmission, and duplication of any of the content found herein, including any specific or extended information, will be done as an illegal act regardless of the end form the information ultimately takes. This includes copied versions of the work, physical, digital, and audio unless express consent of the Publisher is provided beforehand. Any additional rights reserved.

Furthermore, the information that can be found within the pages described forthwith shall be considered both accurate and truthful when it comes to the recounting of facts. As such, any use, correct or incorrect, of the provided information will render the Publisher free of responsibility as to the actions taken outside of their direct purview. Regardless, there are zero scenarios where the original author or the Publisher can be deemed liable in any fashion for any damages or hardships that may result from any of the information discussed herein.

Additionally, the information in the following pages is intended only for informational purposes and should thus be thought of as universal. As befitting its nature, it is presented without assurance regarding its prolonged validity or interim quality. Trademarks that are mentioned are done without written consent and can in no way be considered an endorsement from the trademark holder.

Introduction

The whole world speaks the most primitive language, yet few speak it fluently. Body language is a silent and complex language that has been studied for many years.

4 Commandments for Reading Body Language

Commandment One: Situational Awareness

Observing consciously and attentively is essential to understanding body language. Being aware of your surroundings is indispensable to recognize where you are at all times, having a solid picture of every element and/or person happening around you. You must learn to change the chip from seeing to observing, from hearing to listening.

Commandment Two: Context and Baseline

People have a baseline pattern of behavior. Whether it is walking a certain way, looking too much or too little in the eyes, tendency to cross their arms, certain gestures, gestures, even moving the foot up and down while sitting. A change from this baseline, depending on the context, can tell us a lot about what is going on in a person's mind.

Commandment Three: Changes What Never Changes

Be situationally aware of inconsistencies between a person's baseline, words, and gestures. Changes in behavior can indicate changes in thinking, emotions, interests, and intentions.

Commandment Four: From Local to Global

It is impossible to read a single word on a page and know what the whole page says. The same goes for body language, not isolating one gesture (local) from the others (global). Many pseudo-experts misinform when they express that if the person crosses their arms, it is because they are blocked, or other false statements like that. No, you must learn to observe gesture by gesture until you can make a global analysis in order to determine what is really going on.

Chapter 1.
How to Analyze People

Take a moment to imagine a time when the sight of someone sent a chill down your spine. You may not have known why, but you were simply uncomfortable around the person that you were facing. Despite your best attempts to identify the reasoning behind your problem, you found that there was no particular reason that you could discern. The only thing you knew was that you were the only thing afraid of the person in front of you and had no idea how to overcome them.

There was a very good reason for this guttural reaction—your instincts were telling you that something about the other person was not right. You didn't need to know specifics, and all that mattered to you was that your reactions were accurate. This is because all these guttural reactions must do keep you alive. So long as that is managed, your instincts did their job.

There are limitless reasons that being able to rationally understand what is going on in someone else's mind is critical, even if you already have a decent gut reaction. Ultimately, when you can analyze someone calmly and consciously be aware of why you are uncomfortable or what is putting you on-edge, you are better prepared to cope with the problem at hand. This is because you can act rationally. You can strategize on how to better react in the most conducive manner that will allow you to succeed in the situation.

This means that in the modern world, when things are very rarely life or death situations, making an effort to switch to responding rationally and consciously is almost always the best bet. You will be able to tell when someone is setting off your alarm bells because they seem threatening, or because they seem deceptive. You will be able to find out what the problem is to respond appropriately.

Why Analyze People

Analyzing people is something that is utilized by several people in different capacities. The most basic reason you may decide that you wish to analyze someone is to understand them simply. When you have an in-built technique of understanding others, you will discover that having a cognitive instead of an emotional connection is critical to establishing a true connection with someone else's mind.

Consider for a moment that you are trying to land a deal with a very important client. You know that the deal is critical if you hope to keep your job and possibly even get a promotion, but you also know that it is going to be a difficult task to manage. If you can read someone else, you can effectively allow yourself the ability to know what is going on in their mind truly.

Think about it—you will be able to tell if the client is uncomfortable and respond accordingly. You will be able to tell if the client is being deceptive or withholding something—and respond accordingly. You can tell if the client is uninterested, feeling threatened, or even just annoyed with your attempts to sway him or her, and you can then find out how to reply.

When you can understand the mindset of someone else, you can self-regulate. You can fine-tune your behaviors to guarantee that you will be persuasive. You can make sure that your client feels comfortable by being able to adjust your behavior to find out what was causing the discomfort in the first place.

Beyond just being able to self-regulate, being able to read other people is critical in several other situations as well. If you can read someone else, you can protect yourself from any threats that may arise. If you can read someone else, you can simply understand their position better. You can find out how to persuade or manipulate the other person. You can get people to do things that they would otherwise avoid.

Ultimately, being able to analyze other people has so many critical benefits that it is worthwhile to be able to do so. Developing this skill set means that you will be more in touch with the feelings of those around you, allowing you to assert that you have a higher emotional intelligence simply because you come to understand what emotions look like. You will be able to identify your own emotions through self-reflection and to learn to pay attention to your body movements. The ability to analyze people can be invaluable in almost any setting.

How to Analyze People

Though it may sound intimidating, learning to analyze other people is not nearly as difficult as it may initially seem. There are no complicated rules that you need to memorize or any skills that you need to learn—all you have to do is learn the pattern of behaviors and what they mean. This is because once you know the behaviors; you can usually start to piece together the intent behind the behaviors.

You can begin to find out exactly what it is that someone's eyes narrowing means and then begin to identify it with the context of several other actions or behaviors as well. You can find out what is intended when someone's speech and their body language do not match up. Body language rarely lies when people are unaware of how it works, so you can often turn to it for crucial information if you are interacting with other people.

The reason this works to understand people is because it is commonly accepted that there is a cycle between thoughts, feelings, and behaviors. Your thoughts create feelings, and the feelings you have automatically influence your behaviors, as you can see through body language.

Effectively, you will be looking at behaviors that people display and then tracing them back to the feelings behind them. This is why body language is so important to understand. When you can understand what is going on with someone's behavior, you can understand their feelings. When you understand their feelings, you can begin to find out the underlying thoughts that they have. This is about the closest thing to mind reading that you can ever truly attain.

To analyze other people, you have a simple process to get through—you must first find out the neutral baseline of behavior. This is the default behavior of the person. You must then begin to look for deviations in that neutral behavior. From there, you try to put together clusters of behaviors to find out what is going on in the mind of someone else, and then you analyze. This process is not difficult, and if you can learn how to do so, while also learning how to interpret the various types of body language, you will find that understanding other people could never be easier.

When to Analyze People

Analyzing people is one of those skills that can be used in almost any context. You can use it at work, in personal relationships, in politics, religion, and even just in day-to-day life. Because of this versatility, you may find that you are constantly analyzing people, and that is okay. Remember, your unconscious mind already makes snapshot judgments about other people and their intentions, so you were already analyzing people, to begin with. Now, you are simply making an effort to ensure that those analyses are made in your conscious mind so you can be aware of them.

Now, let's take a look at several different compelling situations in which being able to analyze someone is a critical skill to know consciously:

In Parenting

When you can analyze other people, you can begin to use those skills toward your children. Now, you may be thinking that a child's mind is not sophisticated enough to get a reliable read on, but remember, the child's feelings are usually entirely genuine. In essence, they have their feelings that they have, and though the reason behind those feelings may be less than compelling to you as a parent, that does not in any way dismiss the feelings. By being able to recognize the child's emotions, you can begin to understand what is going on in your child's mind, and that will allow you to parent calmly and more effectively.

In Relationships

When you live with someone else, it can be incredibly easy to step on someone else's toes without realizing it. Of course, constantly stepping on the toes of someone else is likely to lead to some degree of resentment if it is never addressed.

Yet, some people have a hard time discussing when they are uncomfortable or miserable. This is where being able to analyze someone else comes in—you will be able to tell what your partner's base emotions are when you interact, allowing you to play the role of support.

In the Workplace

Especially if you interact with other people, you need to be able to analyze other people. You will be able to see how your coworkers view you, allowing you to change your behaviors to get the company image that you desire. Beyond just that, you may also work in a field that requires you to be able to get good reads on someone in the first place.

In Public

When you are interacting with people in public, you need to be able to protect yourself. When you can read other people, you can find out whether you are safe or whether someone is threatening or suspicious. This means that you can prepare yourself no matter what the situation is to ensure that you are always ready to respond.

In an interview, you may find that read an interviewer's body language can give you a clue on when to change tactics or move on to something else. You will be able to tell how you are being taken simply by watching for body language and other non-verbal cues.

In other words, you deem the person speaking authority and therefore deem them to be trustworthy. Instead, make an effort to see the other party as what they truly are by learning to read their body language. You can tell if the politician on television is uncomfortable or lying simply by learning to analyze their behaviors.

In Arguments

When you are arguing with someone else, usually emotions are running high on both ends. No one is thinking clearly, and things that were not meant can be said. However, when you can analyze people, you can start to find out when someone else is getting emotional to disengage altogether.

In Self-reflection

When you can analyze other people, you can start to analyze yourself as well. This means that you can stop and look at your body language to sort of check-in with yourself and find out what is going on in your mind. Sometimes, it can be difficult to identify exactly how you are feeling, but this is the perfect way to do so in a pinch. If you can stop and self-reflect, you can identify your emotions.

In Self-regulation

Identifying your emotions then lends itself to the ability to self-regulate. When you are, for example, in a heated argument and feel yourself tensing up and getting annoyed, you may be able to key into the fact that you are getting annoyed and respond accordingly.

Chapter 2.
How to Learn Speed-Reading People

Speed-Reading is a technique to increase reading without compromising understanding and retention of information. There are several different methods of Speed-Reading, but they all aim to read clearly, but faster.

For those who work as a freelancer, especially the producers of web content, digital marketing, etc., reading is a prime activity. And Speed-Reading lets you take even more of the time you have available for this activity. It is through reading that you deepen your knowledge to argue more strongly and keep your repertoire of subjects relevant and up to date.

Unfortunately, it is not always possible to devote the time needed to complete reading an article or a book. In this situation, Speed-Reading helps you extract the most important information in less time.

What Is Speed-Reading?
Speed-Reading is a technique that seeks to increase the reading speed without compromising understanding and retention of information. There are several different speed-reading methods for both books and online texts and they all aim to read clearly as well as faster.

Check out this step by step guide and learn how to enhance your speed-reading skills!

1. Train Your Eyes to Make Bigger Jumps

Do you know how the movement of your eyes works while reading? Basically, it's a jumping move. Your eyes pin one point on the line and then jump to the next.

The higher this leap, the more proficient is your reading. Beginner readers, like children, skip only one word at a time and therefore take longer to finish each line. Therefore, the first step of Speed-Reading is to train the eye movement so that it is wider.

2. Go Straight Ahead

The second step is to control that anxiety, that sense of obligation to understand 100% of the text. We are going to take this up further, but know that 80% understanding is an excellent goal.

In other words, you do not have to return to the beginning of the page every time you do not understand a line. After all, re-reading can take a long time—and that is precisely what we are trying to avoid.

Besides, you can fully understand the general idea of a text, even though some excerpts are more confusing. Then, after finishing the text, resume only the parts where you have doubts. But if you stop and go back constantly, you will never finish reading.

Another important tip is not to interrupt the reading to check the dictionary. If you are very curious about the meaning of a word, write it down to check later. However, do not abandon the text to browse the dictionary because when you return, it will take you even longer to resume reading.

In the meantime, try to understand the term by context—you may not absorb the exact meaning of the word, but it will be enough to understand the message the author wanted to convey.

3. Stop Speaking the Words

The third step is to eliminate a negative practice that is a habit of many people: to pronounce the words as they read, either loudly or mentally.

This habit prevents the development of Speed-Reading because it means that you will literally read word for word.

The speed slows down and as incredible as it may seem, the capacity for understanding as well. Because your brain will be busy with pronunciation, you will not be able to concentrate on interpreting what you are reading. The result is that you will have to reread the same stretch several times.

If you are too accustomed to pronounce as you read, losing this habit can be a difficult and time-consuming process. An interesting tip is to put a pencil in your mouth as you read. With a little practice, you will lose this "craze" and see how it improves your reading time.

4. Use Skimming Technique

The fourth step is "skimming." This is a well-known technique for Instrumental English, but it is also useful for Speed-Reading in any language.

Skimming consists basically of looking quickly through a text to extract basic information—index, title, and author, date of publication, main subject, subtopics developed, graphics, and images.

This technique is useful for you to quickly evaluate any text and then set whether to devote more time to a full reading.

If you are researching a specific subject, for example, skimming will allow you to identify whether a particular article or book has relevant information about the subject. Besides, you will find the excerpts that interest you more easily.

5. Use the Scanning Technique

The fifth step, "scanning," is another technique used in English Instrumental. It consists basically of looking at the text to identify keywords, which in this case are relevant terms, related to the information you want to extract from that content.

Suppose you are reading a twenty-page article on People Management, but the subject that really matters to you is Productivity. In that case, you do not have to read all twenty pages, which will certainly tell you about various other issues that are not important to you right now.

Instead, just look through the article for terms directly related to productivity, such as "time," "organization," "concentration," and so on. When you find one of these terms, you just need to read that passage. Thus, you quickly get information that is of interest to you and "skip" the rest.

6. Monitor Your Performance

Once you incorporate what you have learned in the first five steps, the evolution of your Speed-Reading will depend on practice. But to see if it's working, you need to keep track of your progress.

So, the sixth step is picking up a timer and monitoring how many words you read per minute. As a reference, keep in mind that a typical reader reads, on average, 150 words per minute. Meanwhile, a good speed-reading practitioner can read up to 800 words per minute.

But do not just monitor speed. Take into account, also, the use of reading, that is, how much you can understand the text without having to return to it a second time. Your goal should be an average of 80% utilization.

Remember that there is no point in speeding up reading, and thereby lessening the understanding of what has been read, as the re-reading also represents a waste of time.

7. Train Your Focusing Ability

Now that we've covered the best strategies for Speed-Reading itself, let's take a few tips that will enhance your reading experience as a whole and as a result, help you absorb more information in less time.

The ability to stay focused while reading is critical to being productive and not wasting time. The deeper you "plunge" into the text, the better you understand what the author wrote.

What happens, then, if you go to every two paragraphs to check the notifications on your cell phone? The experience will be interrupted and continually resumed, which diminishes your ability to comprehend and thus takes you to take more time to understand what is read.

In this way, you waste twice as much time: the extra time it takes to understand what you read and the precious minutes wasted with distractions (Smartphone, computer, social networks, etc.).

If you often suffer from it, the key is to turn productivity into a habit. To do so, when you read, keep the distractions away. This means not leaving the phone nearby, not keeping the computer by your side, and, if possible, turning off the internet or at least placing your devices in airplane mode.

This time is for you to dedicate to the text and nothing else! The more you can focus on reading, the better your ability to practice Speed-Reading.

8. Find a Quiet Place to Do Your Reading

The place you choose to do your readings also greatly influences the speed and dynamism of the activity—something very connected to the danger represented by the distractions, as we just mentioned.

Noise from traffic, from work, from an establishment (such as a bar, for example), and even from music can disturb your ability to concentrate, making you frequently "quit" reading. Also, if you are reading in an environment with other people, you will also be directly interrupted if they speak to you, even if it is a quick dialogue.

Besides being silent, it is also important that the chosen corner for reading is comfortable. When you are comfortable reading, it is much easier to indulge in the text and devote your full attention to it. And if you have a special space where you like to read, another advantage is that this will make it easier to establish reading as an integral part of your routine.

9. Do Not Insist When You Are Tired

You may have heard that it is not very productive for a student to spend the night studying for a test that will be given the next day. At that point, the desperation of a few extra hours of study is no longer as important as the rest, which will allow more focus and better memory for the student during the test.

The same principle can be applied to Speed-Reading. When we are tired, regardless of whether the exhaustion reaches our site and/or head, our ability to concentrate decreases dramatically. You will find yourself having to read and reread the same passage several times, and of course, it takes much longer to read each line.

And the worst part is that the next day you can pick up the text and realize you cannot remember much of anything you read the night before. This is because a tired brain also decreases its ability to retain information.

So, an important point of Speed-Reading is to know the time to stop.

10. Read Whenever You Can

What the reader does not like to sit in their favorite armchair and deliver hours and hours to a book or even a relevant and high-quality text? However, as you well know, this is not always (or rather, almost never!) possible.

Does this mean, then, that you are bound to a routine? Of course not! It turns out you do not have to self-punch yourself for not being able to devote several hours of each day to reading.

Start enjoying every free minute, especially with regards to idle time spent in queues, waiting rooms, or on public transportation, for example. And how about going a little early to bed, every night, and reading before bed?

A block of fifteen or twenty minutes in which you would do nothing when dedicated to reading becomes time well spent. With this, you advance much faster in your readings, although you cannot read much each day. Another advantage is that this will help you build the daily habit of reading—and, who knows, it will even encourage you to separate a few hours of your day into the activity.

Do you already practice Speed-Reading? What is your Speed-Reading achievement? If you have not yet reached the goals proposed here, do not worry. Reading is a habit you cannot be afraid to develop, and the benefits are gigantic.

Chapter 3.
Understanding Deception and Deceptive Tactics

Deception is a hot topic in today's society. At the root, deception is making claims that are false in nature, which leads people to believe an idea or concept that isn't true. Deception comes in many forms, from propaganda to simple conversation, from the aggressor to the victim convincing them of something false. In today's society, we are faced with deception at all angles. Some of the ways we are regularly deceived include:

The Media

Often times in the media we are given half-truths instead of the full picture. These half-truths lead us to complete the idea on our own. This is often used when it concerns public offices, racial inequality, world events, and even your local weather.

Food

With labels reading everything from no hormones added to healthy and fat-free, we are unable to fully discern what we are eating and what the real regulations are.

Religion

For some, religion is a huge contention of deception. Whether it's the belief as a whole or the misinterpretation of religious text.

Personal Relationships

When we are deceived by the ones we love, it is hard to believe anything anyone says anymore.

The Interpersonal Deception Theory was developed by David B. Buller, and Judee K. Burgoon, both communication professors. At the time of its inception, deceit was not considered an actual form of communication. The IDT is an attempt to relate how people handle deception at both a conscious and an unconscious level. To fully understand deception, you have to know some of the forms in which it is presented.

- Misinterpretations of the Truth
- Downplaying of the Truth
- Stretching the Truth
- Holding Back All the Information
- Contradiction
- Ambiguous Statements
- Lies

People and larger entities use deception for many reasons. The three main motives for deception include avoiding punishment or protecting someone or something to keep relationships intact and to preserve the aggressor's self-image. On top of those motives, things like propaganda and media acts of deception can oftentimes be linked to larger goals. For example, a country might put out propaganda to trick the people into believing that everything is okay, or that another country is the enemy when there is no truth behind it. A media outlet may put out misleading or half-truths to broaden their base of supporters for a specific cause or political candidate.

In today's political market deception can be found across party lines, both in the media and directly from the sources. It is a game of back and forth, telling mostly half-truths for you to draw your own conclusion based on your predetermined political ideals. These half-truths can lead to separation of the people and battles back and forth within the community based on political thoughts and notions.

On a smaller level, deception from person to person can lead to broken relationships, financial loss, loss of property, and even death. There are also forms of visual deception. They come in both nature and through human-made efforts. Disguises are another form of visual deception. As you can see, many of these types of deception are for survival purposes. It is when they move into personal gains or selfish reasoning's that they become dangerous across the board.

Detecting deception can be difficult, especially when the deceit has no real grounding in physical proof. You could have him/her battle, and the only proof is the words being spoken. How then is one supposed to know which side is deceitful and which is telling the truth? Oftentimes these decisions come down to your personal viewpoint and how well you know the people that are telling you the possibly deceiving stories. Other times, as it is with media and propaganda, research can be done to find out what the entire truth is.

Beyond the boundaries of nature, psychologists have studied deception for many years. They have cataloged, listed, and researched the different types of deception and what the psyche behind it holds. Those with a high likelihood of using their dark psyche often turn to deception for personal gain and to hold onto the lifestyle they have created.

The Psychology of Deception

Deception, boiled down, is essentially lying. Whether the truth is only half the truth, or the information is twisted to fit an agenda, it is a lie. But how often do we find ourselves lying? While no one likes to admit that they have lied or lie regularly, it is a regular part of life.

Bella DePaulo, Ph.D., a psychologist at the University of Virginia, conducted a study in 1996. The study used 147 people ranging between 18 and 71 years of age. Each person was asked to keep a journal of all the lies that they told during the course of one week. The study had the following findings:

- Most people lie once to twice a day.
- Men and Women, equally, lie in a fifth of their social interactions that last more than ten minutes.

- In the course of one week, both sexes deceive thirty percent of the people they interact with face-to-face.
- Some relationships attract deception more than others.

While we grow up being taught that lying is bad, and telling the truth is always the best way to go, as adults we don't follow that rule at all. Even some of the most influential professions such as lawyers, accountants, and politicians lie and deceive on a regular, or even daily, basis. Oftentimes, lying keeps you from receiving punishments. For example, if you are late to school, telling them that you overslept will give you detention, but telling them there was an accident will usually let you off the hook. For such small insignificant occurrences, we are pressured into lying not to pay unneeded penalties when nothing is changed by our lateness.

DePaulo's study also included breaking down the types of lies, and the types of relationships most affected by them. She found that couples that are dating lie to each other about a third of the time. Most couples lie from the beginning about things like prior relationships and sexual history. Within marriage, the lies go down to about ten percent, and usually about small everyday things. DePaulo stated, "You save your really big lies for the person that you're closest to."

There are other types of lies as well. The small lies we tell others to avoid hurting their feelings. When we tell someone we like their new haircut or the color of their new magenta shoes. We tell people that they are good people that their mistakes don't define them when we know they often do in our society. People with extroverted personalities tend to lie more, especially when under pressure. We also, when facing mental health issues such as depression, tend to lie to ourselves. Those lies can go either way. We can deceive ourselves into thinking everything is fine, or we can further dwell in our own pits of self-loathing, creating lies about ourselves that drag us down further.

The cold hard truth is that we, as a society, have set boundaries and expectations that are rigid enough that every single person lies. Most people, put under enough pressure and fear, will lie about anything. Some deceive to hurt others. Child custody court is a very good example. The father gets up and makes up complete untruths about the mother to discredit her. The only thing the judge listens to are the words from both parents and has to decide which one is being deceptive and which one is not. This can often highly affect a child's life.

With all the ways around things these days, what is the real reason that we lie? If there is an easier way to avoid discontent and deception, everyone should use it, but we don't. We use lies to put out the fires in our lives quickly, only to find out those lies often start new ones. It is an endless cycle that everyone has gone through in their life.

Top Ways to Effectively Deceive

If you really want to know how to be an effective liar, the answers are all over the place. First, sit and think about a time you have been lied to, but the liar was terrible. Think about the things that were dead giveaways to you. It might have been body language, it might have been their inability to repeat the lie, it could have been filled with absolutely ridiculous information that anyone would have known was a lie. Whatever it is, take note of that. Those are things you do not want to make the mistake of doing. Beyond knowing what not to do, there are several things you want to make sure you always have in line before lying.

Reasoning Is Everything

By reasoning, we don't mean your motive. Reasoning means, is it worth it? Pathological liars have a mental condition that triggers something in their brains that is almost a reward for telling a lie. Most pathological liars no longer have any idea what they are saying, and whether it is truth or lies. They will lie about anything at any time for no reason. To be good at the deception you basically have to be selective. Keep your lies to a minimum. This wills not only save you from having to remember all of your lies, but it will also create a persona of trustworthiness so when you do lie, no one will really question it. Pick the best times to lie, the times you will get the most out of it.

Have Your Story All Laid Out

There is nothing worse than telling a lie and then having someone ask questions, especially when you don't have the entire story and all the details laid out ahead of time. Making spur of the moment decisions on your stories can often lead you down a bad path.

Things don't line up, timelines are off, and lies don't seem to fit together. On top of that, all of the lies you told spur of the moment now have to become cemented into your mind. You have to remember what story you told. To have a fluid deception, you have to lay out your story from the beginning to the end. Look at it from an outside perspective and think about all the questions that could be asked. Integrate that information into your mind and then test it for inaccuracies. Compare it to any proof that might be brought forward.

Create a Lie That Is Not Completely a Lie

There are always some truths to lies. One way to get around getting caught in a lie is to tell the truth but leave it short storied. Allow the other person to conclude based on how your lie is told. Give a false impression when you tell your truth, one that pushes the other person in the direction that you want to see them go. Creating a lie from a truth will also help to avoid questions that can significantly increase your ability to carry out your venture successfully.

Chapter 4.
Narcissism in a Relationship

Making a sweeping generalization about human characters can be improper due to the random nature of humankind. Spotting a narcissist needs a keen eye since such persons hide the real faces behind humor and empathy. They can easily attract with first impressions like good looks and conspicuous kindness than can be felt by anyone. This could however be a welcome to a very stressful relationship, a relationship full of emotional sabotage and deceit.

Contrary to what somebody might think, narcissists, can fall in love just like other people do. The true identity of a narcissist in such a case unleashes itself slowly as time goes by. The relationship will then get more toxic from time to time, giving a partner a hell of an experience. A partner can lose self-esteem due to mistreatments coming from the narcissistic better half. For this reason, narcissistic relationships are prone to breakups.

Some of narcissism cannot be hidden, its toxicity can easily be observed. Individuals in this class have their real faces on. They behave as their reasoning, so they are as they should be. Such individuals have been seen to be attracted to sensitive and empathetic people against the odds. This could be against the will of a person in the question, but that is a natural fact as far as narcissistic relationships are concerned. The observation is, however, quite ironic on how someone will fail to identify the narcissist to prevent bad experiences in a precious lifetime.

The manifestation of narcissism in a relationship can vary according to the factors such as, when both people are narcissists, another factor is when one partner is behaving in a way that can cause damage to his/her better half. The first factor can rarely be seen but it can happen, partners cannot just simply let go of the factors besides true love. The latter can actually be observed in many cases now; it is evidenced by myriad abusive relationships that have been witnessed among the couples. Bad things done by a narcissist could be being center-minded, putting his/her needs before the better half's significant needs.

Signs of Narcissism in a Relationship

They Often Make One Feel Guilty

They are good at manipulating, and will often try to make you feel discouraged and guilty for reasons brought about by them. They have a way of making you feel sorry for things they have even done themselves or minor reasons. They will blame you for reasons that would just have themselves to blame, they are also known for looking for small faults and making it look like you really did a big mistake.

They Are Manipulative

A narcissist is a kind of person who will have nothing standing his or her way in acquiring what they want. Such people would want to make you fit in a position in assisting them to achieve their goals. Making you serve roles that you wouldn't have wanted for your personal reasons. Such manipulation automatically comes upon the narcissists because they regard themselves as special and as people who are full of confidence in themselves.

Entitlement

Narcissistic disorder seems to grant some of its victims a strong belief that they will have somebody do what they ask. That they can command and through you, all that they want will be accomplished. They find their own needs more important than those of their partners and should be met without any delay. That forms abusive relationships over time, making their partners experience dreadful experiences in love life.

They Seem to Defy Some Rules That Apply to Everyone

Due to so much felt self-importance, narcissists act like some rules should not apply to them. They are seen to push ahead of their colleagues regardless of the gatherings at public places like they do not value the rest. Under this factor, they are also known for standing against anyone regardless of the ranks. To elevate their esteem, narcissists step on everyone in the manner in which they do things, they consider themselves special and thus they should have their power and control validated.

Frequent Threats

This is also a true sign of a narcissist; it is associated with a high temper. Somebody who pours threats like 'I didn't need you anyway, you can leave me alone' could likely not be so promising in the long period relationship.

Externally Impressive

Narcissists have a common way of making themselves appealing, be it in their social lives, possessions, or in their general body appearance. They often do a thorough cover-up of their true selves, they can blaze in the eyes of beholders but deep down they are enormous social misfits. This factor relates to the others above in a sense that most narcissists have a feeling of self-importance, making them feel above others. They make this feel like it should be an acceptable fact by making themselves look quite impressive. It however does not alter anything about them.

They Believe They're Very Special

If somebody thinks you cannot live without him or her, then beware you could be in a relationship with a narcissist. Narcissists value themselves with a high degree of specialty compared to others. Such guys believe that nobody can do something better than them. The worse aspect of this factor is that they expect you to feel them equally as they feel about themselves. They do not want to feel challenged or underrated, so they can only go a long way with partners who can comply with this, even if by pretending.

Hot and Cold

They are good at seducing people to win something they need. They can sweet-talk through compliments and other possible means to win favor from you. Feeling great through praises is how many people's hearts are won. The narcissists however can switch from being so good to a nasty mood, to make you feel discouraged and guilty, to have you carry blames for some things you didn't do.

Narcissistic Abuse

This is the abuse associated with the relationships of a narcissist. It is a form of emotional abuse from narcissistic individuals to people who are close to them. Besides psychological and emotional abuse, there are other forms of abuse grouped as financial, spiritual, sexual, and physical. The following are relationships in which the above mentioned narcissistic abuse manifests itself.

Workplace

Research shows that abusers often get an easy way of getting up the ranks at the place of work, winning the trust of their colleagues. Their impressions give them an upper hand in achieving such since most of them are considered smart, thus more deserving than their co-workers. Gaining dominance over others is what narcissists go for; they follow this up regardless of the path they use. They are psychopaths who can play workmates against each other, they then stand to gain favor from all the directions to reach where they want to in the company. Such a trait has been observed to be dominant among the managers than the rest of the workers of the lower rank.

After achieving their 'deserved positions' in the company through the co-workers, they then use intimidation and harassment to push others down. Undermining others is also another way they use to put down the rest of the workers, earning a feeling of overpowering them. As far as Workplace Bullying Institute is concerned, these are the sources of domestic violence at the place of work where an individual with narcissism trait is the only beneficiary. Their acts conflict with the morals, but they often seem not to care as their objective to clinch the positions of power.

Parent-Child

Family relationships keeping people together as parent-child or among siblings makes the perfect environment for narcissistic abuse. For instance, a parent who is a narcissist will demand power to control and feel self-validation, which will be imposed on their children. A child's misbehavior is seen as outrageous disobedience of the parent's direct orders. The parent feels utterly neglected the slightest provocation, developing hard feelings, which is associated with bad things such as corporal punishments.

Love Relationships

Narcissism is born from self-esteem and a feeling of entitlement of an individual. In the case of a narcissistic partner feeling less admirable to their partners, they will in turn demean the looks of their partners. They belittle the looks of their lovers to make them feel better or just above them. Their natural ultimate goal here is to boost their ego over their partners, and this is how to make themselves suit their standards.

Their annoying tactics go as far as humiliating their partners in public places. They enjoy the emotional reaction from their victims when they make them feel guilty and humiliated. They can literally behave like sadists, in this case, practicing what is termed as gaslighting, making their victims feel at fault and annoyed even before the gatherings. This is their way of how to take and seal control and power over the rest of the people that are their partners involved.

A narcissistic love partner will demand to be valued highly, to have his or her grievances addressed in good time, and be well-attended to. Frequent threats to the partner is another outcome of a narcissistic relationship. The partner with narcissistic traits will want often to have the other partner feel guilty and discouraged, even for the wrongs they have caused. They are associated with turning the guilt to their partners; they dig the dirt on a partner to make them look bad.

Fear and anxiety will always be a portion of a partner in narcissistic relationships. The behavior of a narcissistic partner is unpredictable, good times are just but a short lift, they make one feel wanted and well valued but then, they can still bring regrets in the next minute. They're often regarded as bright and classic people, judging from how present themselves socially, physically, and economically. Ironically, they are people who are not able to create and guard strong social relationships even with their own lovers.

As explored earlier in this article, narcissistic individuals tend to disrespect their mates by putting their needs before others' needs;

in a love relationship, they will obviously make a partner feel intimidated. They will be felt as uncaring and too many toxic partners for a smooth relationship. This is a reason to why a person in a relationship with a narcissistic individual will often beadvised to abandon the relationship as soon as possible.

Narcissism and Healthy Relationship

The traits of a good relationship can vary from one couple to another. It is fitting to bring a contrast between a relationship full of conflicts and that of a healthy relationship in this article. Some features of a healthy or rather what could be termed as a good relationship are discussed.

Respect for Each Other

People in a relationship need to show positivity to build a good relationship. Treating each other well is the core of this factor; this should be despite frustrations somebody could be going through. Differ peacefully if you must differ to allow room for a better tomorrow of a relationship. This is to avoid the distress that is associated with narcissistic relationships easily.

Chapter 5.
Victims of the Narcissist

You have finally found someone that appears to be not just wonderful, but amazing. The first couple of months are nothing short of magical. You have a seemingly perfect relationship. Of course, there are a couple of bumps here and there that appear to be red flags; however, you let it go, as to whom in the world doesn't have a bad day. You don't believe that they intend to be so mean. Aside from that, they apologized. However, it appears that you have been the one doing most of the apologizing.

It is difficult for you to pick out what it is you did wrong; nevertheless, you apologize anyway since that's easier. They tell you that you activate their moodiness, but they never let you know exactly what it is you did not do, nor do they tell you why it had them so upset. You notice that they appear to be quite secretive about a lot of things.

Before you know it, things escalate. They get furious for no discernible reason, and you two break up. You ask for another chance, or they might beg you. The relationship is back on, and then it all begins all over again. This individual is an emotional parasite. This is the sort of person who takes advantage of the kindness you have and hopes to exploit it in the worst way. You know deep down that this person is not for you, but it is difficult to leave, as you feel the desire to stick with someone that has previously been through a lot.

The truth is, none of this is your fault at all as narcissists are best at emotional predating. You have likely heard of Narcissistic Personality Disorder; however, the truth is an individual does not have to exhibit the full traits of Narcissistic Personality Disorder to have the traits of narcissism. These types of people are dangerous to be around. It might even seem that you did not get involved with them; they more likely got tangled up with you. One moment you are flirting with a person you believe is excellent and the next thing you know you are involved in an extraordinarily committed and intense relationship, with no way of discerning how exactly it happened.

This is because narcissists are known to be survival masters. It is almost as if they can sense and identify people that are more likely to fall prey to the side of them that is charismatic. They are also able to sense people that are likely to hang on and ensure that they are taken care of especially after they have revealed their true repulsive selves. This is where knowing how to handle a narcissist will help you to eradicate their existence from your space.

The question is, how do you identify the signs associated with Narcissistic Personality Disorder? If you can recognize the characteristics listed below in yourself, it could be that you have a higher likelihood of being besieged by a narcissist.

The truth is: "There Is Something in Your Possession That Narcissists Want: Power, Money, Lifestyle, and Position."

When it comes to a relationship that a narcissist is tangled in, there is usually an inimitable dynamic in play. It always begins with a catch, a dream perhaps. It is often one that you believe is about you; however, it is solely controlled by the narcissist.

There are times when the narcissist might appear to be helpful, only for things not to work out, and they flip the script on you. The moment you catch on to their tricks or attempt to make them accountable is when tension escalates. Having learned that below are the kinds of individuals narcissists love to prey on:

Conscientious people

One of the most noteworthy qualities that narcissist search for is the capability of being conscientious. Conscientious individuals are preoccupied with the well-being of others, and they are likely to see through any obligations they have to others. Considering decisions are made using their morality, they are more likely to accept as true that the narcissist operates on their own moral compass. This causes them to believe that the narcissist will see through their obligations as well. Narcissists understand that when their targets are sufficiently conscientious to concern themselves with the well-being of other individuals, they can take advantage of that quality for their own selfish purposes.

Malicious predators understand that a conscientious individual is bound to believe them, even if they appear unsure and are more likely to give them another chance. They also know that these conscientious individuals care about the needs of the narcissist, even if it is at their expense. This type of caretaking, narcissists recognize, is linked to the responsibility that is created by a romantic relationship. This causes them to trust that these individuals will go out of their way to fulfill their obligations to them.

People with Empathy

For a narcissist, having a target that is empathetic can never be understated. A narcissist can't receive a steady dose of resources, attention, praise, and more from any individual that lacks empathy. While narcissists lack empathy themselves, they search for targets that have a hefty dose of empathy. Narcissists use an empathetic individual as emotional fuel to make themselves feel in control and powerful. If they do not get this emotional fuel, they begin to starve and search for a new source.

This trait is used to take power away from victims in a cycle of abuse. Narcissists count on the fact that you can see their side or their view, even if they are abusing you. This is what keeps the abuse cycle going. An extremely empathetic individual is an ideal candidate to listen to their pity ploy of abusive events.

Narcissists believe that once they provide a fake apology or a sob story, the abuse can be erased. This is because they understand that you, being an empathetic individual, will rationalize their conduct and make justifications for them. They depend on you being able not only to forgive but empathize with them, especially after the terrible events of mistreatment. When they appeal to your empathetic side, they can evade being held accountable for their behavior, every single time.

Empathetic individuals tend to rethink their decision to have the narcissist held accountable, as they feel an inordinate amount of culpability the moment the narcissist is being punished. What they do instead is to be compelled to try to protect the narcissist rather than have them deal with the consequences of their true self being exposed.

People with Integrity

An individual who keeps their promises can be a desirable proposition to a narcissist. People like that have a host of characteristics that narcissists believe they can selfishly exploit. This is because it is not like an individual with integrity to cheat in a relationship preemptively.

Narcissists tend to feel almost no regret for causing their victims harm, however, their victims, due to their morals, feel apprehensive when it comes to retaliating or relieving themselves of the obligation or making a conscious effort to betray the relationship. It is this integrity that offers them a benefit when in a relationship with like-minded, empathetic individuals that becomes ammunition for the narcissist. It is what they use to destroy any iota of trust they have in the world.

People with Resilience

Being resilient is being able to recover from an abusive event. This is something that strengthens the emotional bond of a victim with the narcissist. Individuals like child abuse survivors are known to be resilient, and they have provided an infinite source of victims for narcissists as they are capable of withstanding quite a lot of pain. While this is a beautiful trait to have in life when it comes to confronting everyday adversity, in an abuse cycle, that resilience becomes a weapon wielded by the narcissist to ensure that their victim remains ensnared in their world.

Afterward, highly resilient individuals are not likely to pack up after abusive events, even though they might have an increased ability to recognize abusive threats. They usually choose to ignore any instincts they have and instead fight to save the relationship. This stance causes them to adopt a fighter or savior mentality while they attempt to save an extremely unsustainable relationship. They might even choose to measure the love they have by how much cruelty they can withstand. This could also be down to the type of trauma bond they have developed with the abusive and toxic person.

Extremely Sentimental People

An individual who is not only sentimental but loves deeply is one that appeals to a narcissist, as they can use excessive praise and flattery to groom their victim. This is done to appeal to the individual's desires and needs easily. Narcissists choose to idealize their targets very early in the relationship, and this enables them to use their target's need for love to gain their trust. Narcissists love to create memories that are happy early on, as they know those memories will be romanticized and used for comfort during the relationship's abusive periods.

A narcissist enjoys messing with their target's emotions. What they do is intensely mirror the emotions their targets show before they start to withdraw. This is done to create a faux soulmate effect that leaves their targets drained and addicted. Empathetic and sentimental individuals are the perfect candidates for narcissists to manipulate, as they have to exploit the target's need for a proper relationship.

People Who Were Raised in Dysfunctional Environments

It is important to note that one's previous experience can make it quite challenging to recognize boundary violations the moment they happen. This can cause you to disregard your instincts when your trust is violated. Narcissists do not like limits. If you are unable to set them or keep them, this is a weakness that a narcissist can exploit to their benefit. There are times when narcissists will act like heroes; however, instead of encouraging empowerment or independence, they use that as a means to build dependency.

People with a Frantic Need to Be Loved and Are Lonely

A narcissist lives by the motto; look for a need and fill it. An individual that has low self-confidence can be controlled easier than someone that is extremely confident. Initially, the intensity will feel great as it is confused for passion; however, a narcissist is unable to be transparent. The initial intensity begins to wane, revealing a cold and calculating disposition that makes you wonder what you did wrong and how you could locate the loving individual that you met at the beginning of the relationship.

People Who Accept Blame Willingly

As the relationship begins to wane, narcissists begin to guilt-trip you and claim that you are the delinquent one in the relationship. Sensitive and empathetic individuals are very vulnerable to blame due to their naturally reflective disposition. When a narcissist redirects your attention to something you seemingly did wrong, they divert attention from their own unhealthy behavior.

Chapter 6.
Attraction and Manipulation - Put This in Correlation

Some people are natural at reading others, but they couldn't tell you how they know what they know. That's because they are intuitively reading others' body language, but they don't have the knowledge to define why they are such good communicators. More than 70% of the messages we send and receive are through non-verbal language. Not only are the greatest percent of our messages non-verbal, but that non-verbal language is more honest and genuine than the words we speak. Our bodies don't sugarcoat the message; we just respond and react without being conscious of doing so.

If people are saying one thing, but their body language is delivering a different message, put more stock in what you see than what you hear. However, to make sure you are reading the person correctly, let's discuss all the different non-verbal messages we send. We'll cover the non-verbal signals and what they might mean, but keep in mind that different cultures and countries might attach a different meaning to your body language. When you're confused about the non-verbal message that another is sending, then listen to the words and take the signals in context with the phrases they use.

Another way to determine the message is through the tone, pitch, and volume of another's voice. It gives truth to that saying, "It's not what you said but how you said it." When all these things are examined during your analysis of others, you'll find clarity in the message. While we're at it, there is one more thing—pay attention to the other person's required personal space. If you are questioning whether the message they are sending is positive, negative, or benevolent, step inside their personal space and be aware of their reaction. Their feelings will then be quite pronounced. If the message was meant to be off-putting, they will immediately step back or adopt a space-claiming stance that will let you know their feelings in no uncertain terms.

Facial Expressions, Features, and Head Movement
Playing with Hair and Moving the Head

If someone slides their fingers through their hair at the temples and tosses their head back, this is an indication they might be flirting with you. On the other hand, if they are running their fingers through their hair from their forehead through the top of their crown, that is a sign they are confused or frustrated. Tilting the head and twirling the hair is also a flirtatious mannerism, indicating interest combined with a little nervous tension.

When people nod their heads, it matters how many times they do so before stopping. For example, public speakers who are attentive to their audiences know that three nods mean interest and attentiveness. However, if you observe a group of people conversing, you'll notice the person who nods their head only once is eager to leave and will probably be the next one to make a quick exit.

If someone is interested in what you're saying, they will often tilt their head in your direction. They could be showing curiosity or questioning what you are saying when they bring one ear closer to make sure they are getting every detail of the conversation.

Eye Movement

People usually blink six or seven times a minute, but those who are stressed blink quite a bit more. If someone covers their eyes with their hands, excessively rubs their eyes, or closes their eyes, they could be hiding something or feel threatened. When the eyes are shifty or rapidly moving from one person to another, it reflects some scattered thoughts that are going on in their heads. If there is a flickering interest between two people when this is happening, then it can also be a way for people to prevent detection as they were checking out the other.

If someone has a habit of not making eye contact or looking down as they speak, it can show shyness or can also be a cry for empathy. They are waiting for you to ask what's wrong and open the way for them to share their feelings. Investigators have come to realize that a sustained glance from a person, who denies involvement in a crime, may mean they are lying and trying to over-compensate by looking them straight in the eyes for a long time to show they're telling the truth.

If you have asked a question and the person you asked looks upward, they are most likely trying to picture something they saw. On the other hand, if they look to the side toward their ear, they could be trying to recall a message they heard. If they look downward after your question, they are connecting your question with something negative and trying to find a way to avoid answering or revealing their feelings about the matter.

Eyebrow Movement

If individuals raise their eyebrows, it usually means the person is curious about or interested in your conversation. A quick pop-up of one eyebrow could be a flirtation, and if the eyebrow is raised a bit longer, it often means that the other person doesn't quite buy into what you say.

If the brows furrow, you can almost bet that person is having second thoughts about what is being done or said. It most likely indicates a negative emotion like fear or confusion, so it might be time for you to back off a bit.

Lips

Of course, a smile sends a universal message, if it is truly a smile. We've all been at the other end of a fake smile, which is one that doesn't travel all the way to the eyes and makes them wrinkle in agreement. We call those "Red Carpet" smiles. They are Hollywood smiles given by people who are trying to be friendly to their fans but just want to get inside, sit down, and make it through the night.

Individuals, who plaster a smile on their face almost all the time, are usually nervous. If it's in the workplace, they could feel out-of-their-depth or incompetent. There's a good chance that foreigners who smile a lot don't understand a blasted thing, so they just smile and nod.

Another thing people do with their lips is to suck on them and bite them. Sucking or biting the lip is a reaction by those who need to settle themselves down. Like a newborn, the action soothes them and offers a bit of comfort in a stressful situation. If one clamps down on their lips or purses them, it can mean frustration or anger.

Body and Limb Movements

Body Positions

If there is a group of people standing and talking and one or more people open their bodies to you, that is an invitation to join the conversation. If they just turn their head, you might want to choose another group. You will know if you have captured the attention of a love interest because he or she will turn slightly toward you and point their feet in your direction, to indicate they are interested in finding out what makes you tick. If you step into the group and the person beside you touches your shoulder or arm, this is a direct ploy to show you they are interested in exploring the relationship a bit further.

When you step into the group, if the person beside you leans in to you, they genuinely like you. If their head retracts backward, perhaps something you said surprised or offended them. If they physically lean away from you, they've already made up their mind that they're not going to listen to or like you. If they turn their head in the opposite direction and follow it with their shoulder, you just got the cold shoulder. So, forget about it!

Standing Positions

If someone is standing with legs about shoulder-width apart, it often is a sign of dominance and determination, as if they needed to stand their ground against something or prove a point. If they stand with legs together, front forward, they will hear you out, but you need to make your point quickly. When the person you are speaking with is standing and shifting their weight from side-to-side or front-to-back, it might indicate several things. They could be bored, or they are anxious and need to soothe themselves with this rocking sort of movement. To determine their feelings, it is necessary to look further at what they are doing with their arms as well.

Arm Positions

Don't assume that crossed arms always mean that the other person is upset. Not so! Some people will stand or sit with their arms crossed because it is just a comfortable position. You can distinguish the other's emotions by looking further at their facial expression. If they have furrowed eyebrows, their mouth pursed, and their arms crossed, chances are they are angry or upset about something. Crossed arms can also be a sign of protection or a closed attitude to the ideas you are presenting.

If someone is talking with their arms flopping around, it can mean they are excited and agreeable, or it can say that they are out of control. Again, you'll need to couple your observations with other non-verbal messages to be sure. Typically, people who are overly animated are less believable and have less control over their emotions, as well as having a lack of power. They flail their arms to gain attention as if to say, "I'm talking now, so would somebody please listen to me?"

Leg and Foot Positions

People whose toes turn inward could be closing themselves off to your comments, or they could just be pigeon-toed. To determine if there is a physiological issue that causes their toes to point it, you might need more background information. Don't rush to judgment, just wait, observe more body language, and listen to their words. Some people, who began turning in their toes because they were insecure or awkward, might have created a habit that they find difficult to break. The only message they are sending is one that says; I have a physical issue that is impacting my body language.

Sitting Positions

If a person is spread out all over your couch, they have a feeling of self-importance. On the other hand, they probably have a good deal of confidence as well. Legs open, leaning forward with elbows on knees shows an in-charge attitude that is still open to hearing what you have to say.

If a person is sitting next to you and crosses their legs at the knee, pointing their foot toward you, they are permitting you to approach them. If, however, they are sitting next to you and angle their body in the opposite direction, you're probably not going to engage or connect with him or her. If that same person is fidgeting, quickly moving their ankle or foot, they are looking for a way out. Excuse yourself; both of you will probably feel more comfortable.

Chapter 7.
Understanding Emotions

Emotions are key in emotional intelligence and as such, we should be able to understand them better to know what we feel. Not only emotions are vital to emotional intelligence, but they play an essential role in how we behave and think. What we feel every day can compel us into taking action and influencing our decisions that have to do with our lives, no matter how large or small.

For you to truly understand emotions, you must first understand the basic components of emotion which are the following:

- How you experience an emotion - the subjective component
- How does your body react to emotion - the physiological component
- How you behave as a response to an emotion - the expressive component

Emotions can last for a short amount of time, such as a fleeting annoyance at your coworker, or they can last for a very long time such as sadness over the loss of a meaningful relationship. However, what is the role of emotions and why do we feel them?

To start with, emotions can motivate us into taking action. For example, when a student has to deal with a difficult exam, he or she may feel a lot of stress and anxiety about whether he or she will do well at the test and how this test will impact the final grade.

Due to these emotional responses to stress and anxiety, the student may have a higher chance to study hard for the exam. Since the student experienced a certain emotion, he or she had been motivated to take action and make a positive step to improve his or her chances of having a good grade.

People also take action to experience positive emotions and lessen the risk of feeling negative emotions. For instance, you may wish to go out and socialize or indulge in hobbies that offer you happiness, excitement, and contentment. On the other hand, you most probably avoid getting yourself in situations that might lead to anxiety, boredom, or sadness.

Emotions are also able to help us avoid danger, thrive, as well as survive. According to Charles Darwin, emotions are adaptations that permit animals and humans to reproduce and survive. For example, when we are angry, we are more likely inclined to deal with the source of our anger. When we are afraid, we are more inclined to get away from the threat. When we feel love, we are more inclined to find a mate and reproduce.

Emotions are also able to help us make decisions. Our emotions greatly influence the way we decide whether it is what to eat for breakfast to which candidate should we vote for in elections. Also, according to research, people who suffer from certain types of brain damage that affect their ability to experience emotions face difficulties to make good decisions.

Even during the times when we think that our decisions are made based on rationality and logic, our emotions still play an important role, as is the case with emotional intelligence that has been shown to play an essential role in decision-making.

Emotions are also the ones that allow other people to understand us. When we interact with others, it is important to offer them clues to help them understand the way we feel around them. Such clues may have to do with body language, like the use of facial expressions that are connected with the certain emotions we feel at that moment.

In other cases, we may directly express how we feel. For example, when we tell our family members or friends that we are frightened, happy, excited, or sad, we offer them important information they can use to take action and respond to us.

As a result, emotions are also used as a way for us to understand others. In the same way that emotions are used by other people to understand us, emotions are also used by us to understand others. Social communication is part of our everyday life and relationships.

As such, it is essential to be able to understand and react to the emotions other people project. It offers us a way to appropriately respond and create more meaningful and deep relationships with our friends, family, and other important people to us. Emotions also allow us to indulge in ineffective communication during different social situations, including our work. Charles Darwin has also suggested that displays of emotion also play an important role in our survival and safety. For instance, if you were to encounter a spitting or hissing animal, you would understand that the animal is defensive and angry and as a result, you would back off to avoid any potential danger.

Our emotions exist to serve a wide variety of purposes. However, completely understanding them can be a tricky business. The way we feel our emotions and the different ways we react to them makes us unique.

Psychologists have tried to identify the various types of emotions people experience. Throughout this process, different theories have emerged that explain and categorize the emotions that people feel. Psychologist Paul Eckman during the 1970s he proposed six basic emotions that as he suggested were experienced universally in all human cultures.

These emotions are:

- Happiness
- Disgust
- Sadness
- Surprise
- Fear
- Anger

Another categorization of emotions was created by psychologist Robert Plutchik, who presented the "wheel of emotions." According to this theory, emotions can be combined to form different feelings in a similar way that colors can be mixed to produce different shades. The basic emotions act as building blocks while more complex emotions are only blends of these basic emotions.

To both theories, basic emotions remain the same. For this reason, let us take a closer look the some of the basic emotions as well as analyze their impact on our behavior.

Happiness is maybe the only emotion that people strive to achieve the most. It is often defined as a pleasant emotional state that includes feelings such as joy, satisfaction, well-being, joy, and contentment. This emotion is often expressed in the following ways:

- The pleasant tone of voice
- Facial expressions like smiling
- Body language most commonly with a relaxed stance

Even though happiness is believed to be a basic human emotion, the things we consider it will create are influenced by culture. For instance, the influence of pop culture emphasizes getting things such as having a high-paying job or buying a home as ways of attaining happiness. However, in reality, the various things that will contribute to being happy are more complex and have to do with each person separately.

For example, for a long time, people believe that happiness and health are inherently linked with research supporting the fact that happiness can play an important role in mental and physical health. It is linked with increased marital satisfaction and longevity.

On the other hand, unhappiness has been linked to various poor health outcomes. For example, depression, loneliness, anxiety, and stress have been connected to lowered immunity, decreased life expectancy, and increased inflammation.

However, severe and prolonged periods of sadness can lead to depression. Sadness can be expressed in the following ways:

- Quietness
- Dampened mood
- Lethargy
- Crying
- Withdrawal

The severity and type of sadness varies and depends on its cause, as well as how people cope with these feelings. Sadness is known to lead people in indulging in various coping mechanisms such as ruminating on negative thoughts, avoiding other people, or self-medicating.

Such coping mechanisms will actually enhance the feelings of sadness and prolong the situation.

Fear can be a powerful emotion that plays an important role in our survival. When we come across some sort of danger, we experience fear and our bodies start a process known as the fight-or-flight response.

During this response, our muscles become tense, our mind is more alert, and heart rate, as well as respiration, increases, preparing the body to either run away from the danger or fight it. This is the response that helps us make sure that we are ready to deal with threats in our environment effectively. Fear can be expressed in the following ways:

- Facial expressions like the widening of the eyes
- Physiological reactions like rapid heartbeat and breathing
- Attempts to flee or hide from the danger

Fear is not experienced by people the same way, with some being more sensitive to it and also particular objects or situations being able to trigger this emotion easier than others.

Fear is our emotional response to an immediate threat. We can also have a similar reaction to expected threats or thoughts that have to do with potential dangers. This is what experts commonly refer to as anxiety. For instance, social anxiety has to do with an expected fear of social situations.

On the other hand, some people actually seek out situations that will cause them to be afraid. Take extreme Sports for example and other similar things that can induce fear. This is happening because some people seem to enjoy and thrive when under such feelings. However, when we are exposed to fear repeatedly, it can lead to acclimation and familiarity, which can reduce feelings of anxiety and fear. This is the basic idea behind exposure therapy, during which people are exposed in a safe and controlled manner to the things that scare them the most. As time passes, the feelings of fear will start to decrease.

Another basic emotion as described by Eckman is disgust that can be shown in the following ways:

- Physical reactions like retching and vomiting
- Turning away from the thing that disgusts us
- Facial expressions like curling the upper lip and wrinkling the nose

The revulsion we feel during disgust can come from various things such as an unpleasant smell, taste, or sight. According to research, this emotion was developed as a reaction to foods that may have been fatal or damaging. For instance, when people tasted or smelled foods that have gone bad, their typical reaction was disgust.

Another example can be that a disgust response can be triggered by poor hygiene, blood, death, infection, and rot since this may the way our body is telling us to avoid such things that may carry diseases.

People are also able to experience moral disgust as they observe other people involved in behaviors deemed evil, distasteful, or immoral.

Anger is another powerful emotion that includes feelings of agitation, antagonism towards other people, hostility, and frustration. As is the case with fear, anger can also play a part in the fight-or-flight response of your body. The threat can generate feelings of anger, and as such, you may feel inclined to protect yourself when you fight off the danger. Anger can be shown most commonly through:

- Body language like having a strong stance
- Facial expressions like glaring or frowning
- The tone of your voice like yelling or speaking gruffly
- Aggressive behaviors such as kicking, throwing objects, and hitting
- Physiological responses like turning red or sweating

Chapter 8.
Being Proactive

Finally, it's going to be incredibly crucial for you to be proactive. The biggest failure that you will have as a leader is simply not doing anything at all. Even If you make the wrong decision and have some mistakes. That's still better than sitting around and just hoping that everything changes. It is up to you to take action and get the things that you want from this life. Lead by example. Always reflect and grow and make sure that you motivate your team by listening to them and building their emotional intelligence.

Leading by Example

The best method of leadership that you are going to want to use is to lead your team by example. You can't tell people what to do, only for you to not follow the same rules in return.

Not everything that you want your team to do is something that you need to tell them directly by using your words. You can show them how to act by the way that you perform. What we need to remember about leading by example is that they are also the one who's responsible for actually teaching people how they should be responding and respecting you in any given circumstance.

Make sure that no matter what happens, you are never afraid to get your hands dirty and do the hardest tasks of the day. While you don't have to do this every day, if you are always giving everybody else the challenging things that they don't want to do, then it makes you look bad as a leader. Many people assume that just because they are the manager, they've earned their rank and that means they no longer have to do some of the most laborious work there is. While this is true, in some cases, you do still have to make sure that you are willing to get down and dirty with the rest of your team.

It doesn't mean that you won't be doing the most laborious tasks all the time, but remember that even though you do have a higher rank, you are still getting paid more in the end. For many individuals, it is their business as well. So, if you are a leader who owns their own business, then you can't expect people to work for you and do some of the hardest things. When you are the one making the most money and not as willing to participate in these more challenging tasks, remember that what you act on is always going to be more of a sign of who you are and what your character is, rather than just the simple words that are coming out of your mouth. Actions will always speak louder than words.

Make sure that you are practicing active listening as well. Too many individuals aren't willing to fully listen to others, and will instead do all the talking. You need to open the door for communication for your team, which means actively hearing what they have to say while sharing important information as well. Every conversation should include two people; it shouldn't just be one-sided. It is not just about telling things to other people. Make sure that you are always giving people freedom, as well. If you want to create independent and thoughtful team members, then you have to be the type of person who lets them take the lead every once in a while and take action for themselves. This is going to create autonomous and responsible adults, who, when put together, will make an incredible team for your company. Always be the person that you want your team to be. Always show who you are in a way that makes your team able to see exactly who they should be. You are a leader, which means that you will have followers. You aren't just the boss telling people what to do. It is up to you to keep the team together. You are the strong independent glue that holds everybody along with your high morals and integrity.

Reflecting and Growing

Hopefully, by this point, you have a higher ability to be able to self-reflect.

That doesn't stop there. However, your journey is not over. It is just the beginning. Every day going forward, you should have a period where you can self-reflect. Maybe it is why you are taking a shower, as you fall asleep, or when you are driving to work. Wherever it just takes a minute to ask yourself a few questions to make sure that you are really creating an objective perspective of yourself.

Ask yourself what your biggest mental challenges might have been recently. Are you more stressed than usual? Is anxiety getting the best of you? Do you have trouble managing your anger? What is it that you've been struggling with? Make sure that in the same breath you criticize yourself; you also ensure that you are looking at the benefits of your skills. Is there anything that you are proud of about what you have accomplished that has made you a better person?

Are there things that you've achieved that you never thought you would? Also, make sure you reflect on your relationships. Are you a good friend? Are you the right partner? Are you putting in the same work that other people are? Is there anything that you need from other people? Are there things that other people might need more from you? Look at yourself, reflect, and find things that help you to understand better the way that you are interacting with yourself with this world, and with everybody else that you know.

Motivating Your Team

As a leader, it is also your job to make sure that you are the one who's motivating your team. We should all be teaching our team how to drive themselves, but at the same time, we must ensure we know how to do those ourselves.

No matter what you do, always thank your team. Make sure that they feel entirely appreciated and that they know how thankful you are to have them there.

Whenever somebody has a new idea or concern with you, always take it on with enthusiasm. Be incredibly appreciative that they trust you and those they feel open to expressing their true feelings to you. Have open communication and make sure that everybody can say what's on their mind. You need to use enthusiasm and compassion with them as often as you can. Be excited that they have new ideas.

There are a few essential things that you can do to ensure that you are consistently motivating your team and other ways. Make sure that you give them tasks that might be a little bit harder than what they're typically used to. Encourage them to do this and tell them that you will be there to support them along the way. Give them all the tools that they need to complete these tasks successfully. By giving them harder things, you were showing them that you trust them and that you believe that they are intelligent and capable human beings and make them feel good. It helps provide them with a little boost of confidence. Ensure that you are also giving them the chance to be creative when possible. While the task might not involve total creativity, it is also something that they might be able to put their own personality or voice into. Throughout this entire process, make sure that you have one-on-one time with them. If you never really get to know somebody or speak to them face to face and they can feel disconnected from you. You want to allow them to form a healthy and robust bond because this is what is going to keep them motivated and connected to your workspace.

Increasing Listening Skills

You are going to be managing people and delegating tasks. One of the most important things that you will do as a leader is listening. Listening is easy. All you have to do is sit there and hear the words as they come into your ears. However, not everybody is an excellent listener. Too often people are planning what they're going to say next, rather than listening to what somebody is saying. Now, to be the best listener possible, remember that it is not just about hearing what words they're saying. You also have to look at the context of the situation. Consider their emotions and personality. What might they be thinking versus what they feel comfortable saying to you? There's always going to be a deeper meaning and unspoken words that should be part of the overall truth. Here are a few listening tips that will make it easier for you to show others that you care about what they're saying.

Ensure that all distractions have been put away and that you are facing them one on one, maintain eye contact, and let them know that you are there to listen to them and support them. Repeat what they're saying back to them to make sure that the way that you comprehend it is the same way that they are trying to express themselves. Don't overdo the attentiveness. You don't want to stare at them directly in the eye the entire time. You don't want to have frigid body language. Be open and relaxed and have it be a casual conversation that you might have with a friend.

Make sure that you restrict any judgment. Even though you might not be saying things, it might show in your face if your brow is scrunched up, or if your mouth is open, or if you have a generally confused look on your face. You don't want to scare them into keeping things from you because they feel as though you are judging them too harshly. Give them a chance to have a moment of silence before you respond. Sometimes they might not be done. Or they might want to reflect a bit on what they just said to make sure that it is actually what they genuinely move. Ask more questions to pull as much information as you can from this. You don't want the conversation to earn and have to revisit it later on by asking questions that should have been discussed the first time around. If you have to take notes, it will actually show them that you really care about remembering the things that you are talking about. If you are managing a large team, you might forget individual small bits of information that are shared throughout the day, especially if you have multiple meetings at a time. Taking notes means that you can reference things, that you have a record that you were listening to, and it shows them that you care about the things that they're sharing. Actions will always speak louder than words. So always remember to consider that what they're saying is critical, but what they're doing is also something that we have to evaluate.

Conclusion

Now the time has come to immerse yourself in real life, to experience its variety of possible situations. Your daily activities will be your laboratory, and your current and developing relationships will be your experiments. You now have enough knowledge to advance your studies. You will find that the more you use your abilities and hone your instincts, the greater your skill will be. All skills require development, and reading body language is no exception. A good idea is to share your newly acquired knowledge with those closest to you, as well as with those who may be against you. Keep in mind, too, that by understanding body language, you can use it in many ways. We hope you will use the information you have gained to respond better to those around you and to work with others to solve problems effectively. You now know that a person is much more than what they say with words, and sometimes even more than what they communicate with their facial expressions. This concept alone will make you more aware of those around you, which, at the same time, will make others feel more appreciated and better understood by you. The result will be more effective and positive communication with everyone in your life.

www.ingramcontent.com/pod-product-compliance
Lightning Source LLC
Chambersburg PA
CBHW062150100526
44589CB00014B/1771